NEW LIGHT FOR
THE OLD DARK

NEW LIGHT FOR THE OLD DARK

Sam Willetts

CAPE POETRY

Published by Jonathan Cape 2010

4 6 8 10 9 7 5

First published in Great Britain in 2010 by
Jonathan Cape
Random House, 20 Vauxhall Bridge Road,
London SW1V 2SA

www.rbooks.co.uk

Addresses for companies within The Random House Group Limited can be
found at: www.randomhouse.co.uk/offices.htm

The Random House Group Limited Reg. No. 954009

A CIP catalogue record for this book is available from the British Library

ISBN 9780224089180

The Random House Group Limited supports The Forest Stewardship
Council (FSC), the leading international forest certification organisation.
All our titles that are printed on Greenpeace approved FSC certified paper
carry the FSC logo. Our paper procurement policy can be
found at www.rbooks.co.uk/environment

Mixed Sources
Product group from well-managed
forests and other controlled sources
www.fsc.org Cert no. TT-COC-2139
© 1996 Forest Stewardship Council

Typeset in Bembo by Palimpsest Book Production Limited,
Grangemouth, Stirlingshire

Printed and bound in Great Britain by
MPG Books Ltd, Bodmin, Cornwall

to Flora

'All may yet be well'
H.T.W. (1922–2005)

CONTENTS

NEW LIGHT FOR
THE OLD DARK

ANCHOR RIDDLE

My first baptism readied me
for those to come:
the water roared,
receiving me.
My lines sing
mast, hull and spar,
the cold furrow I plough,
the bones that lie under.
I have a woman's symmetry
but I am double-male.
My curving reverses
the great curve I resist.
Muscled and cocky,
my badge has sweated
in striped Marseilles;
off Petersburg, I cracked
the fog-white winter palace.
Hope is my hanger-on;
ocean's barbed emblem,
I am crossed memorially
but I hold a ring, here,
best man
in the wedding of the sailor
to the sea.

STROKE CITY

(Derry, 2001)

Silks of cloud and sun slip
across the mountainside.
The estuary is a bright hook

sun-fishing. Down on the rock,
a cormorant, like an undertaker
flashing, keeps vaunting

the black shab-splendour of his breast.
Under the cannon on the military wall,
the Bogside is laid out: a soldier's dream,

a map scaled 1:1. Observe the history
of peat-smoke rising from a chimney,
the halting of a car at the junctions

on that homely uncompromising grid.
Outside the shops, my friend Paul,
Bogside-born, says *Look at the floor*:

the pavement's overlaid solid
with pale-coral, ivory, dove-grey
chewing-gum. *Welcome to the city*

of the grinding jaw.
Behind us a watchtower
bristles, stuck thick

as an African nail-fetish head
with suspicious devices. Permanent
numb hard-on of an intimate war.

TRUANTING

Masculine, feminine, neuter:
beside boyish reaches of the Thames
I watched horses, companionable
strangers to impatience, switch at summer
head-to-tail. By the little-sister river,
spring calves jostled, saint-francissed me
to keep on scratching the pink
and humble itch between their ears.

A pinched-out cigarette stank in my palm
while I sang *Trouble in Mind* to the mule canal.
At night, I knew the lines shone
like a river of rails under the sidings-lights
as the wake of a train broke gently
through my bed; by day, the sleepers
were steps laid flat to their vanishing-point,
each track a ladderback *A* for *Away*.

FUR-SORTING

In the lit corner of this vast shed I work
like the rats by touch and smell as well as sight:

even the best synthetics crunch between
your fingertips, but real fur parts

down to the aromatic hide, spreads
as it would have when the living animal stood

exploring the wind. A low sheen runs across
silk-cursive legends – *Silvermann*

New Bond Street Guaranteed. Revenant
scents from collars and linings trail long-forgotten

assignations. The nearest thing to warmth here
is the radio's lost bonhomie, swallowed into

the dark. Sometimes the bad light yields
little shocks, like the dainty snarls on those four

foxes stitched into Siamese-quads; then my
own hide pimples, horripilates in sympathy.

The furs love lapsing from their pallets, to flood
the concrete in a lavish slump; some pieces,

somehow, keep coming back – that whole bear's skin,
macabre, scurfed with grit and sawdust, clacks

its claws like sad maracas every time.
Darkness of year's end and a mound of rags

remade daily. The radio yatters to the freezing air. Deep inside the fur mounds, pink litters squirm for life.

ST COLUMBA'S FOOTPRINTS

(aboard the MV Claymore)

The missionary sailors
threading these shouldered islands

in blind weather had only their own silence
to save them, listened as one man

for the breakers of a wrecking shore.
Tonight, in this dark wheelhouse, radar

wave-crests glow and fade between us
and the long pulse of Jura. Out on Davaar

a driftwood cross is lashed outside
the cave that holds a Christ crucified

in oils and drowned twice daily;
at Kintyre, a saint was rowed ashore

whose weight of purpose sank heel and toe
into the rock as if it had been snow.

A CHILD AT THEIR PARTY

1969 from the sun-branded end
of a Victorian garden. Chestnut shade,

jasmine tea lukewarm in willow-pattern,
yellow wine sun-mulling

on a middle-class Dionysian lawn:
a scene from a children's book written

by adults for themselves. From a hammock
between apple-trees, she murmurs

*you're a beautiful child, children are
so beautiful*, laughs *suck!* when I blow

through her cigarette, launching sparks.
Soon, bored of the wrenchable grass

printing my elbows and the sun my eyes,
I open a story-door: out of the heat,

into a kitchen. As it unglooms, the walls
are stencilled always with forget-me-nots.

SMALL GIRL IN A CROWD

Her mother's scratchy cooking-scented pleats
brush against her cheek as she hopscotches

from cobble to kerb in time with the *links-rechts*
crunch. All around her, half-intimidating,

half-protective, is an adult mass of overcoats
and furs, tobacco-smoke, cologne. Her sightline

is level with the scissoring X of breeches
and jackboots, the human machine-hinge.

She senses the stirring certainty and arrogance
of those heels' hacking-down, watches

the steel carapaces flow past shining
dully like wet cobblestones, senses

her mother's fear and scorn. She steps out
from the crowd again and her mother

yanks her back by the hand, so hard
the wedding-ring pinches. Looking up,

eyes narrowed in reproach, she sees
her mother's gaze is far beyond her reach.

TWO-UP TWO-DOWN

Downstairs, mother and young daughter
kitchen-clattering in bright saris,
the clean youngest son home in his school-rig,
ambience of warm mutton fat
and Bollywood rejoicings from the video.

Upstairs, behind the sacred filthy door,
the two older brothers are snake-basking
in the caramel rays of their all-night sun
with their scales and weapons and clingfilm,
black teeth and void pinhole eyes

always scanning yours for treachery,
without ever quite meeting them.
The frantic ring-tones, regally ignored,
the piles of heartbreak cash. And between
these worlds, always calm, the father

(like a solicitous pimping concierge)
who might have dabbled once
in the old country, who nods and murmurs
'*Come, come,*' most graciously
as he waves you on up the sweating stairs.

ON THE SMOLENSK ROAD

The Stukas, finished with the men
and tanks, turned back for the civilians –
the mile-after-mile of refugees scuffing
and trundling behind the Russian retreat

and bottlenecked before a bridge
over the Dnieper. The cocked gull-wings
were sighted, the panic warning yelled
along the line, and everybody ran,

cowering, hands on heads
into the roadside fields.
One woman hit the ground, pulled
down her small daughter, who was

my mother, and whose guiltiest memory
it became. She saw at once that her mother's
flowered dress might make a target, so she
tried to kick, gouge, claw, thrash herself free

from the arms struggling to cover her
from the planes, to bulletproof her with love.
My mother said there was no describing
the insane scream of a Stuka's dive. Was his

blood screaming too, with speed and schnapps,
with young survival, with trigger-happiness,
until he felt like a young sun
firing out of the sun? Perhaps

through his cockpit's panes
he glimpsed some brightness moving
in a small heap below (girl howling
like a dybbuk in her mother's pinioning arms)

or something like a blown flower
out there on the Earth as it tilted, as river
and field and the road's small-and-many
human spillage pivoted away.

THE DANDELION PATH

for my sister

Halfway up the hillside ran a green tunnel, floored
with grass and sheepshit pellets. It was restless-camouflaged:

a childhood zoo for sun and shadow, a leaf-tiger-cage
toothed and clawed in wild striations. It had been let alone

so long it made the new seem old, made the burnt-out
Ford in its gully of ferns seem as old as the ferns, its rust

old as dew, its hubcaps ancient as the curving
of the wind-quiffed oaks. A lifetime's retina-impression:

the hillside, the net of woods that was the sun's roost,
the furrows' tapering-away like the years.

1969 FIN-DE-SIÈCLE

Cinematic, the wintry stripe
of pram-spokes whirring past
the square's black railings
as your baby-blackshoe teenage nanny
pushes by, bombed bright on slimming-pills.
Not far away, Death as a Jaguar
humps onto and down off the kerb,
haunching around a corner towards
All Saints Road and its prey.

High rooms in white houses feel their age,
the caverns below stairs sweat sour chalk,
a touch sick, touch feverish. Fiery
through parted blinds, fiery
over Paddington, with its scorched
orange-peel smell of braking trains,
an optimism is coming
to its famous sunset.

TY CLYD

The Irfon, clear from its troutbrown stones to the sky
and back, splashes out long goodbyes behind
our steps' smack and plunge, wades against our thighs.
We name islands of childhood empire

in aerial survey of rocks rainforested
with moss. Midges stitch the air over
the deeper reach, where chest-high to a child
the surface keeps one scar, undercurrent-marled.

Up on the far bank, never adventured before,
yellow stubble-rows prick at our feet.
The only sign of us – white socks tucked
neatly into our sandals – lies on the warm

home-side shingle. We're missing, trackless –
a mother's God-forbidding dread. Sister and brother
take turns to lead. An electric dullness
over the Brecon hills has set all the leaves guessing;

as the first drops fall, we know that we trangressed
by crossing. We feel our unkindness, our lovedness,
the power of our missing. We pick softly together
through the sharp stalks. We will never be closer.

HONEST JOHN

(John Clare, 1793–1864)

In confinement, imagined he was filling his pen
from an inkwell of his own urine,

saw the pale script fading as it dried
to the invisible ink of his obscurity.

Starving on the run, falls to his hands and knees
like Nebuchadnezzar to eat grass. Keeps

walking back to what does not exist:
long-dead first love, landscape of youth, back

to days before the Sunday best of his brief celebrity.
Thick-fingered daisy-chainer, he knew once

how to become very small, could enter
the tiny world of a ladybird in a high wind,

would read aloud the small names of God
he saw written through the songstruck woods.

Fugitive again, he knows the constellations and takes
their giant word in laying himself head-north, feet-south

to know his way before first light. But first light sees him
far down a wrong road, foul-mouthing the new land

and sky as they spin him in their cock-eyed compass,
misleading him from his way home.

RUBBERNECKERS

He's screaming – You're breaking my neck,
you . . . racist! *racist* mother*fucker!*

Three police-cars, four! Four lots
of blue glimpsers turning in the dusk,

slack knots of gawpers on the corners.
Faced with a wild arrest-resister

the police call in the biggest
lads on this lovely evening's roster:

sweating in stabvests, flushed
like farm-boys at harvest

they bow to their crackling breasts.
Local stones have been disturbed;

Paul and Kelly, crack-rotten, grin black teeth
for me from the half-dark of a door.

The proprietor of the Kashmir Halal,
white-tufted upright squirrel

of a thousand courtesies, *tuts*,
pulls in his young waiter, who's been

loving it and licking his bared teeth;
even two Lubavitschers (his sombre suit,

her modest headscarf) – not being above watching
a man kneel a man's neck to a draincover –

venture from their Chabad House. Yet
the subject, our guttermouth, face down

under the cops, is just a cipher,
already nearly absent,

biro-chewing, paperwork and process.
This event is us, not him: this *is*

community. *My neck, you cunt…*
But his voice is shredding-out anyway,

torn flag in the evening's satisfying
dust and glory. Everybody

lingers, hoping for an encore:
More! is the unsaid buzzed consensus.

Above us all a lone whim of cirrus
breaks into pink, way up

in the blue: perfect, warm and empty
as the corner pubs.

HOME

Near night's end on Dover Docks
the Channel meets the wall in white high-fives

while a wind ramping homeward
pinches my ears goodbye. Unslept,

unshaven, I case the quay, find unlocked
a door to PRIVATE whiteness: tiles, towels,

squalling vitreous enamel. Hot water
sends my face to cloudy-mirrored heaven.

Already not quite England, here – no cock fun
pleas, no race-fatwahs, no glory-holes; not one

good mark of English bog cacography.
Homesickness meets seasickness halfway;

from a rainy sundeck the Channel's swell is
sharp and smooth and sharp again,

repeating, un-repeating.
France lies sunlit in the distance

like a tawny crust, but I keep
looking back at England, riding away shawled

in rain. Great white-walled cake, your dull icing
mined with memories. Sweet, unappetising home.

SAWING

A newly-felled tree-trunk, around my age
by its rings: so this was a new shoot
when I was new. Between each arc
of sawdust wind-fringed from the cut
the blade fast-forwards through
a circle-almanac, opening blond summers
and dark thrifts of winter. Memory
blurs in the push-and-pull,
but snags on this –

my mother reading to me between blue jets
of menthol smoke, and beside us, belly-up
in our summer chair, our Jack Russell bitch
– the one that gave milk
for a blind runt kitten. I cut on
through the years – *re-gret /re-gret?* says the saw –
and somewhere in the blade's return, cut
another day: in the same garden,
with my dad, and burying an old cat
that was once suckled by a dog.

DIGGING

Missionary girl reports that Chinese addicts say
your heart begs you to stay away

even while your legs are carrying you back.
After the merry little jitter of the filter

with the smack, dancing in the spoon, after
the absorbed, assassin-like, childlike procedure –

citric, water, flame – I'm back in the basement,
heartsick, digging for a vein in February

as in a February gone and a February
still to come, spitting prayers through the tourniquet

between my teeth, licking up tears and pleading
for my blood to plume up in the barrel, *please*

blossom up, squid-ink, blood-anemone
in the works – though you can have all that and miss,

or pull out and find you'd *had* a vein, now 'pissing
blood' – Deano's words as his grey fringe smeared across

his forehead, as he missed and bled and raged
to get it IN. Blood: thank *Christ*. Spit out

the tie, inject the welling gratitude,
that flushes pleasure through the grief –

for the help and hope of friends
sold out, for all her loving years –

all of it driven down before one flood,
one gut-bracing stealth of warmth. Ah

well: restorative as sunshine to a snake.
So around the days and the seasons

the junkies go – you might as well accelerate us
till our days and nights are strobing by –

use, cluck, raise, score, use, cluck, raise –
lantern-show flicker of tail-chasing, nameless days

spent waiting, cheating, waiting, struggling to outrun
the burn and freeze and – maybe worse –

the waking-up, to all that's lost: her happiness,
her younger years, the child she might have had.

cluck: cold turkey

WAR STORY

On leave near Naples, Yakub unwraps
and dusts-off his loot: the inlaid chess-table
he's carried all the way from Monte Cassino.
For years he's thought his wife
and young daughter are dead,
cattled into the black trains.

In fact, half-starved but alive
after outrunning the round-ups
and the *Einsatzgruppen*, all the way to Siberia,
they have presumed *him* dead since 1940.
The chance reunion of these Displaced Persons
in safe, rainy Wales, is a freak of joy still years away.
He joked that Naples was even rainier than Wrexham.

A secularised Jew, a jurist, Ashkenazi son
of the Enlightenment, partial to cigarettes
and Latin, a small, tough, clever-eyed,
bullet-headed man, he doesn't drink or gamble,
except on chess.

I see him in his Neapolitan attic-billet, under
a rattling roof. He puts down the chequered table
and tries to pray. Passes his hands over
his stubbled head, and tries, though he knows
that all that will come
is the universal prayer of the rain
answering itself.

YARMULKAH

Never worn, never
lost; gold and silver
thread continuous
through the black.

SANTA ANA, CA, 1956

She holds up her new baby,
a ring shining from her hand that cups

his head, that tender planetary weight.
A white curtain shields them from the sun.

She has on a summer dress, vanilla
gingham *à la mode*, and the strap

slipping down onto her nursing arm looks
like the girlhood she's left behind. Head thrown back,

her eyes and mouth are crescents of laughter,
while glutted in the milk light of her love,

her baby's eyes are blind-hilarious. Outside
in the hot sky, beyond the curtains' swell

a moon inclines; her man's Cold War,
and the hot wars in it, are moon-remote,

untroubling as the hum of the Frigidaire.
High above the city and the desert

mountains, the moon cools, a confection,
a delicious trick, like baked Alaska.

So said Braque
of his friend Picasso,

and Picasso . . . well,
he could fix

a bull in thin air
with a single gesture of fire –

and fix the world
at the same time

with his triumphant
bullseye stare. Talent

pungent as sweat: that reek
of certainty: a magician

roaring effortless
in a fearful cave.

SPRING RECOVERY

Walk the walk, they say here, and now that it's March
I do: through the buds and promises, past the carp
that pout up through the clouds to feed, past

the bandstand crocuses, into
the total sight of the sea:
the unexpectable, the long memento.

My habits have been laid low
by a hard winter's campaign; will they
revive now, and reclaim this spring's recovery?

Walk it, they say, and so I have, into
Ringwood Forest, where a grazing buck
ups his head and freezes me in a half-wild eye,

stands undecided, watchful for my intent.
You're in the right place, they say; *stuck
in fuckin' Chickentown*, says my raging discontent.

WARSAW

Chopin's head was lashed onto
a flatbed car and went for scrap.
Muranow became a neighbourhood of ash,
one spire standing in an urban grate.

Someone spirited Chopin's heart
from the Holy Cross Church before
those aisles and columns prolapsed
across the street in a swelling race of dust.

Christ was laid low, supine on his cross,
head turned aside as if in embarrassment,
nailed hands upraised like a polite request
to be righted; but the soldiers who de-ressurected

Him took snapshots of His slapstick plight.
Copernicus and the rest they punched to dust
with 88s, wiped their hands, ran a book on the hits.
Piwna Street became mad-mountainous,

a ravine of snow-capped rubble. Warsaw was
a thorough job, a *sea of flame*, said Hans Frank,
approving. Strange, how eloquently those snaps
of maimed statuary mourn the desecration

of flesh and blood. But all this all old news.
This is eight o'clock, July, the present day.
The counterfeit Old Town is busy again,
the red sky a new forgetting.

IN HANWAY STREET
WITH PERSIAN ALI

To the west a coast of sky outstrips
the hot coastless city. Beside me
at a beery pavement-table sits

Persian Ali: Zoroastrian, exile, addict,
my graceful-handed acquaintance.
Once a designer of bridges, now

a short-order cook, he's shod in grey
and tie-pinned for the weekend,
his narrow face razored to violet shadows.

Ali admires big women, with a vengeance.
His pupils are vanishing-points,
grey irises wide as the West End pavements.

Soon the sky is history, but a sweat still licks
our lips. One police-car slides by, and another,
slow and self-announcing as a pair of swans.

Now the streetlights burn orange against
the high royal-blue, and I miss you again,
while Ali, scratching, turns polemical:

the Shah   (he says) *you know, Savak, secretspolice,*
they were   never *so bad as these ones now*
– but he smiles into the table's

bright puddle, remembering
cheap abundant opium (I see it
pressed into lustrous sticks like barley sugar)

and the house he built himself
above Tehran
in the beautiful dry hills.

FROM THE DESERT

The Answerer, the young rabbi, high in Kabbala,
humming and rocking, strumming his beard,

the man of all moments answers obliquely
from the blue shade of olives. Flies alight

between his words. His eyes will not blink
under the lashes. He keeps offering

his open palms, as if to say *no trickery*. Mild
as the *clonk* of goat-bells from the valley slopes,

his voice can be heard from far-off,
assuring and explaining. His skin shows

a greyish tinge of sickness and the memory
of the desert stings in his eyes;

out there he saw tall storm-columns teeter
like a plate-spinner's poles as they came on,

fixed his gaze on the way the heat
was shouldering the air on the horizon,

stared into that vibrancy that could be
water, could be anger, could be angels

trembling into this world. He became too still
for Death to see him, waited until

thirst and exhaustion took him and danced him,
pouring into his ears all his Father's purposes.

CROCUSES

Spring, heiress,
has looked this park over;
its borders are vivid
with crocuses.
She'll take it.

GHETTO

After Kazimierz was cleansed, and the wind
had scattered in ash and silvered charcoal

every picture, letter, ornament, cat-and-cockerel
hearth-familiar, a wait began that hangs here still

with the swag of cables over the crossroads
and the pastel washing pegged on balconies;

the streets here wait all day like an early morning
yet to quicken into business, like a one-horse drag

cleared for a showdown that never comes.
Meanwhile, in the polite gloom

of the Ariel Café's pre-war sitting-rooms,
amid the shining of mahogany and rosewood,

it is always late ghetto-afternoon, ominously still,
as if still haunted by the fear of night's train coming.

Too late: the rail spurs have rusted, the household
is long lost. The doilies and silver can only recreate

a homely *Mary Celeste*. Time here is counterfeit,
is repro, since the lives were taken that once observed

these hours, and so it will be as long as Kazimierz
waits for its people to return and fill

the life-shaped emptiness that hangs here,
in the streets, around the synagogue walls,

the shuttered market and the square
in its crooked star of alleys.

NO CHANCE

I last saw you coming
like some terrifying Kali
in the street, moving
in medicated side-effects.
The madness flaring in you
froze me, otherwise
I might have run;

months later,
when I heard you were dead,
I saw you all at once
weak and harmless
as a November wasp,
frailty giant-shadowed
on a bright pane
by a winter sun.

FARMER IN DROUGHT

Dust races
in strands
across the steep
vineyards.
He bends on
one knee to lace
his boot, and
the wind begins
unravelling him:
his dust spins
from his heel
as he stands.

AUGUST 9TH

Down comes the squat black four tons,
dropping silent out of a virgin sky.
Forty-five seconds from release to detonation,

the sunrise-after-sunrise.
Time for millions of unexamined actions,
to finish a cup of coffee, fold your paper,

pay, leave a tip. Time too for countless moments
of conception, or destruction. Still falling;
but when the special gun inside it fires, matter

will fall apart, exponentially: *fiat lux*.
An event so bright it seems to happen many times
at once, racing to the horizons, dazzling the mind,

its moment of un-creation blinding the sun,
blowing out the walls and windows of history.
The plane that filmed this thing was called '*Necessary Evil*'.

GREEN THOUGHT

French windows at the grievous onset
of rain from a sky turned nearly to foxglove,
doves' breasts ruffling along the gazebo parapet,
Bacchus smirking, hoof-dainty, in an alcove;

the whole come-hither, fuck-off patrician vista
undisfigurable by mood or weather,
or by me, tapping ash on marble in the loggia,
muttering *lawn-porn* in a green mental whisper.

NUREMBERG NOTES

Kaltenbrunner, lurching 6'6" SS golem
curls foetal on his bunk, whimpering *please,*
I want my family! Ribbentrop tries
to cop a madness plea: *torture me to death*

in expiation of our crimes! – Don't over-act, old boy.
Julius Streicher, 'uncrowned king of Franconia',
whip-toting, pelvic-thrusting loon, snubbed by the worst,
rattlesnakes at the judges – *Jew-names! You're all Jews!*

In March, young Luise Jodl, soon to be a gallows-widow
sends her *Generaloberst* husband pink-and-white phlox
with a note: *Darling, do not lose your temper with them.*
Outside, an unprecedented winter is surrendering its dead

to the last field-grey Spring. The blinds are drawn
for a two-hour ciné-matinée: horrors seen nowhere before.
'Keitel bows his head. Muted sobs in the court.
Goering leans on his elbow, yawns.'

TOURIST

Warsaw, October: rose-madder by four,
the soldierly grey boulevards slippery

with tickets to winter. After forty years rebuilding,
the Old Town is like this beautiful girl I knew

whose face got wheel-broken in a crash
and remade so well it was hard to say how she

looked wrong. I'd brought with me – holding them
as if they might slip – two questions:

who were my mother's people? where did they die? –
In an attic archive – deep card-indexes, ink turned lilac

with age – I handed my questions to a love-labourer
in a yarmulkah; with sad palms and a shake

of the head he regretted that the answers
now lay probably beyond our reach. So

I abandoned questing and went back to tourism;
joined the *passeggiata*, drank black tea. Got stickied

under sooty lime-trees, saw boisterous children,
all knees and elbows, skyline-capering

on the wall at the river-line. Beyond
their frail silhouettes against the petrol dusk

huge cranes were moving, courtly, confident,
building another new Warsaw across the Vistula.

EROS ON A TRAIN

This track runs tight along the coast,
keeps close to the glancing sea,
past dunes of sparse marram, on
through the timeless aphrodisiac
boredom of a Northern country
in a hot spell. Past two sun-warmed
bunkers: speed-framing, the window
cuts in flickerings of 1940 . . .
rash assignations in a death-quickened
June, rough cloth, cheap buttons,
mouths wind-salted, fine solve of sand
through sand-parting fingers. No
question now: Eros is here, loitering
in this summer carriage, diffuse as smoke,
here in two travelling strangers' looks,
in the belly-flitter of mutuality,
suspense. Two heads turn away, for now,
towards the windows. Out there, a jet needles
through its high other world, its perfect glint
unravelling white across the sky.

DETOXING IN
THE FRENCH QUARTER

As I stepped out of frigid air-conditioning
onto the skillet noon of Bourbon Street
I heard a man's voice *whisht* to me, but turned
to find the sidewalk vacant – nothing there beneath
the balconies but their long griddles
of shadow. Voodoo believers say the dead
may not always leave; sunned-up, I spiked cold again
to think of the Quarter still crowded with others –
its sallow caballeros and darktown strutters,
its long-dead browsers in Cohen the Gunsmith's
and Meyer the Hatter's – an unseen watch
of jealous jazz ghosts glimpsed through wrought-iron,
astir with the vines in the sweet-fried breeze.

FAITHLESS

At this hour, sounds outside are scarce,
so when a motorbike dopplers by
we listen to each other hearing it.

Against your nape my lips move
slow as mountains. I can breathe the past
hours in your hair: they mean our lives

are changed, both compromised. Read me
my mind, tell me what the new day
has found here in your unmade bedroom

where these sweet light-spectres
and cut ambers swim to the wall
through your dressing-table treasures.

JUNE 3RD

You don't stir when I unstick my damp chest
from your back – at that tiny sound,
an orange pulled open, or a kiss
reversed. You've slept through
the window's changes, through its dawning
on me that if I could stay just this far
from sleep, I might escape our years,
somehow make it over those rooftops,
blue in this hour's one blueness – over the drop
to Andy Andersen's backyard, with its litter
of rolled chickenwire, gas-bottles, toys left out;
over it all I'd go looping like a monkey,
from guttering to chimney and up around
that ventilator-stack. If my heels kicked
off a slate, you wouldn't hear it shatter
for your dreams. Sweetheart, you wouldn't
hear me for these birds.
And after that I'd be away,
clear of roofs and city, and moving now
at shaking speed into a day
that's opening like an orchard
and an avenue of that orchard
opening to me like another lover's arms.

A MORAL DEFEAT

(Zydowski Cemetery, Warsaw)

Being taken the long way, the mug's way back
in a minicab (those cheery signs in Krakow –
Auschwitz Taxi – Best Rates!) – I stared at the bristles
of the driver's neck, too tired after ten days
of fruitless searching to argue with those stolid
rolls of fat. Some nerve was paradiddling in my ears;
I recognised it from bullied schooldays: imminent
    tearfulness.

Through the orange rain-reunions down the taxi's window
I went on seeing the Zydowski's evergreen-jungle darkness,
the matted cut-flowers and flooding candle-stumps
that spoke of visits by Righteous Gentiles. The unbearable
wall – privately built, no State money for this – of children's
    faces,
snapshots varnished safe from defacers. I came to these places
to find how sense could be made of it all, and found
it couldn't.

Somehow I got as far as the hotel lobby,
and a brown leatherette banquette, before my
detonation: streaming, snotting, gasping, sometimes
nearly laughing, grateful to be ignored. As soon
as I was able, called another *Best Rates!* taxi
to the airport, to find the soonest flight away.

COUP DE FOUDRE

Free-fall accelerates
at a rate
that's reckoned

as thirty-two feet
per second,
per second.

In Clancy's bar,
her distance like a
closeness beckoned:

thirty-two feet
per second
per second.

HOLT PAUPERS' CEMETERY, NEW ORLEANS

'I thought I heard Buddy Bolden say
"funky butt, take it away, let Mr Bolden play!"'

Far from the tourist honk, cut grass
sweetens the mid-city heat. An old man
called Mr Davies – black D-Day veteran,
his eyes blue-clouded like an aged hound's,

leans, hand-on-kidney, weeding righteous ground.
A scrawl on one lopsided board says
Forever Sadly Misted. Strange aerials, feathers,
scraps of blue protect the Voodoo graves,

and some are furnished: a burst sofa, sodden chairs
of ambiguous vacancy. In a corner of live-oaks
and Spanish moss, the John and Jane Does
(out of the river, off of the sidewalk, says Mr Davies)

sport their wildflower legacies, forgottenness perfected.
Somewhere here, unmarked, lies Buddy Bolden, jazz-inventor,
evicted from his first grave (upkeep unmet). Beads glint
in the trees: voodooberries, wicked-bright. Queen Victoria

still reigned when King Bolden blew in Storyville
and sent his gleaming signature clear across the river
to Algiers. Mr Davies straightens, dabs at sweat, works on,
some blue reward already in his eyes.

SIMON

After ten full years of positive grace
the skeleton keys were turning in his blood;
suddenly his glasses were too big for his face.
He worked on as the sarcoma marks spread
but walked as if meeting a fierce headwind.
On some last day, busy on his daily-made nest
of rags for sorting, he stopped and grinned, said,
I've done some jobs, but I always liked this game the best.

YOU AND ST KEVIN
AND THE BIRDS

To watch a heart being emptied
of trust and desire is to see something
elemental: not a worm's turning
but a tide's. I don't mean you're the redbreast,

or his mate – hardly bird-brained,
certainly not timid. It's just that
any bird I see is yours, the one
from the back of 48, from your lost

family-home; it's the brief superstitious
flights you allow yourself when a robin
or a blackbird, beady on a branch
or quirking-up something from the grass

can for a moment be an emissary,
an affirmer of love's surviving loss,
singing of your dad's unshowy integrity,
your mam's woundings and bitter tenderness,

singing of their watchfulness and care
flitting through your life, their youngest's.
The life that I've been wasting here. And it's
because you went on holding out to me

your stubborn loyalty and kindness
that it's like a laugh, and then no laugh
at all at St Kevin – holding quite still
his palm's unhatched blackbird, never

doubting it will be its own reward.
As sure as the birds are out there

roistering-up a new day, your reward
is coming: a new life will break

in your heart. In a new night, a new moon
that isn't made of scorched tinfoil
will turn your tide again. The birds
are being loud about it.

JEWISH SECTION

Alive, my mother brought me here
more often, perhaps meaning to show me

how grief can find some shape in duty.
We hefted slopping cans from the green tap

by the chapel. On a cold day, the wind
and the massing trees conferred as we stood

at the grave's foot, my hands arranged
in marriage behind my back, my breath

drifting in life-conscious tribute
like the bloom of silent gun-salutes.

Her mother's grave then, now hers too,
and always a cenotaph: its black gloss

golden-lettered in English, Polish, Hebrew
for the majority of her family, whose ashes

fell on birdless woods of pine and birch,
or who were turned, with all those terrible others,

naked and resistless, into Polish earth. Whatever
the lesson of those visits, it didn't take:

wisdom stays away from here, acceptance
stays away, backed off somewhere

behind the wet civic privets and the yews. I
stay away. *The Jews in the yews. Forgive me.*

THAMES TRIOLET

She thought that she might breathe the river,
breathe the river and never rise.
By the lock where brown geese shiver
she thought that she might breathe the river,
lie back from this world forever,
the dim sky closing on her eyes:
she thought that she might breathe the river,
breathe the river and never rise.

TRICK

The unexceptional mystery takes place:
around eleven, love turns to matter, Dad

dead. The ward grows and shrinks, early Spring
breaking promises through the glass.

Dad's untoothed mouth gawps, and its last
O holds one darkness; dark of a worked-out

abandoned mine. His absence is brute
absurdity, his hand soft as vellum.

His new state exposes the stark child of him,
and un-sons me. No answers now to a son's

questions, about this, about the sense,
for all his slightness, of a long life's mass

coming to rest, a settling that churns up
grief in a rounding cloud. Dad

dead; end of the opaque trick
that turns our gold to lead.

STARLINGS

Amazement as we walked together
in the cold of the year – a vast
reach of birds, nearing and ebbing past

understanding, numberless over the fields'
spires of shadow; now like iron filings
magnet-swept in three dimensions,

massing to a dark fold and spreading
light again; now a tidal gesture:
the opening and closing of a hand.

GARDEN

Look to your life.
Rest your kindness
and your unkindness
now, and listen: I know
what makes your heart
clench coldly
in all weathers,
I know how it feels
that it always will.
Bear that. Look to your life,
to your one given garden.

A REDBREAST FLEW
INTO THE KITCHEN

I was fucked, living from hit to hit and floor to floor.
The day after you'd traced me and come round, shaking,
to say you'd met someone, were having his baby,
and I mostly held it together, until you'd left, and your

taxi had gone, and then I pushed shut the front door
and howled like some animal – the day after we'd held
each other in tears to seal our breaking-apart, and I knew
you cared for me, but couldn't have me near your life –

the next day, a redbreast – not any bird, but *that* bird,
your private, Dublin messenger-bird – flew
into the kitchen where I was crashing. Dipped in, perched
at the table's edge, unpanicked, unruffled. Clattered

at no windows, just paused there, bold as truth
and looked at me – looked, *looked* – for a few breaths
and flew clean out again. I sat electrified, heart
banging, nearly laughing at such a plain visitation.

Any resemblance to living magic is purely coincidental.
But thank you, thank you all the same.

ACKNOWLEDGEMENTS

Acknowledgements are due to the editors of the following:

Bridport Prize Anthology, *Granta*, *Identity Parade: New British and Irish Poets* (Bloodaxe), *London Review of Books*, *Poetry*, *Poetry London*, *Poetry Review*, *Spectator*, *Times Literary Supplement*

This collection, of poems written over many years, would not have appeared without the open-handed advice and support of my loyal friend Henry Shukman – thank you. The same *sine qua non* applies to the patience and expertise of Robin Robertson at Jonathan Cape.

Heartfelt thanks must be paid to (among others) Paul Gallagher, Andrew McBride, John and Jill Prawer, Cat and JP, Kate Macintyre, Henry Richardson, Steve Spiegel, Jane East, Matt Sage, Anna Tudor, Jane Bowen, Caroline, Matthew and Anne, Mike and Clare, Rosalind Porter, Steve Thomas, 'Casc' and my sisters.

Also in memory of my parents, and of Charlie Chackas, Hugo Donnelly, Zoë Hornsby, Ivan Tarasenko and Pat Utechin.

Finally, with utmost gratitude to Carol Byrne and her small birds.